PHP Programming Professional Made Easy

By Sam Key

Expert PHP Programming Language Success in a Day for any Computer User!

2nd Edition

Table of Contents

Introduction

I want to thank you and congratulate you for purchasing the book, "Professional PHP Programming Made Easy: Expert PHP Programming Language Success in a Day for any Computer User!"

This book contains proven steps and strategies on how to quickly transition from client side scripting to server side scripting using PHP.

The book contains a condensed version of all the topics you need to know about PHP as a beginner. To make it easier for you to understand the lessons, easy to do examples are included.

If you are familiar with programming, it will only take you an hour or two to master the basics of PHP. If you are new to programming, expect that you might take two to three days to get familiar with this great server scripting language.

Thanks again for purchasing this book, I hope you enjoy it!

Chapter 1: Setting Expectations and Preparation

PHP is a scripting language primarily used by web developers to create interactive and dynamic websites. This book will assume that you are already familiar with HTML and CSS. By the way, a little bit of XML experience is a plus.

This book will also assume that you have a good understanding and experience with JavaScript since most of the explanations and examples here will use references to that client side scripting language

To be honest, this will be like a reference book to PHP that contains bits of explanations. And since JavaScript is commonly treated as a prerequisite to learning PHP, it is expected that most web developers will experience no difficulty in shifting to using this server side scripting language.

However, if you have little knowledge of JavaScript or any other programming language, expect that you will have a steep learning curve if you use this book. Nevertheless, it does not mean that it is impossible to learn PHP without a solid background in programming or client side scripting. You just need to play more with the examples presented in this book to grasp the meaning and purpose of the lessons.

Anyway, unlike JavaScript or other programming languages, you cannot just test PHP codes in your computer. You will need a server to process it for you. There are three ways to do that:

1. Get a web hosting account. Most web hosting packages available on the web are PHP ready. All you need to do is

code your script, save it as .php or .htm, upload it to your web directory, and access it.

2. Make your computer as simple web server. You can do that by installing a web server application in your computer. If your computer is running on Microsoft Windows, you can install XAMPP to make your computer act like a web server. Do not worry. Your computer will be safe since your XAMPP, by default, will make your computer only available to your use.

3. Use an online source code editor that can execute PHP codes. Take note that this will be a bit restricting since most of them only accept and execute PHP codes. It means that you will not be able to mix HTML, CSS, JavaScript, and PHP in one go. But if you are going to study the basics, which the lessons in this book are all about, it will be good enough.

Chapter 2: Understanding PHP Environment, Web Concepts, and Coding Standards

Before going through the technicalities of syntaxes and actual coding, you must understand first the elements of the PHP environment that work together to help create your needed code. In this chapter, you'll learn about the main PHP environment and its vital components, PHP's dynamic content display on browser type, and the commenting styles that will serve as your note.

PHP Environment

PHP needs the right supporting programs to ensure it will work properly. Three elements make up the entire PHP environment:

Database

Database is a platform used for organizing data and data gathering process. The database has a great role in data processing within the system because of its function. The good thing about PHP is it's compatible with almost all available database software. Nowadays, majority of server owners and programmers utilize MySQL, which is a free downloadable database program.

Web Server

A web server is the core computer system that processes network exchanges between the system and the internet. It's in-charge of basic network protocol, which in turn will be distributed across the world wide web. By definition, a web server can be a main computer or a program that monitors and accepts HTTP requests. As a beginner, your current computer is going to be your basic web server that will help you process these requests.

Just like in database, PHP is compatible with any web server application, including paid web server platforms. Apache server is currently a top choice among programmers and web administrators.

PHP Parser

PHP codes serve like the program or operation's backbone. These codes won't make any sense to the average user, but the entire program's operation, navigation, and interface are created through them. Hence, you need a PHP parser that will process HTML output, which will be forwarded to web browsers. For the purpose of practice, you may not need to install a parser for the moment, but you will absolutely need it in the future.

Installing PHP parser should not be a problem due to is simple procedures. Follow the instructions indicated on the PHP guides and see whether you installed them properly or not. To check, type http://127.0.0.1/info/php on your web browser. If it displayed PHP information, then you've installed everything properly. In case you haven't, it will notify you of the possible reason and will give you an idea about how to solve the issue. This is where you need to consult several online guides on how to install PHP properly. Installation procedures across different web server operating system vary. Check your web server version first before continuing with the installation procedure.

Web Concept and Identification

It's been a common question among novice programmers how PHP makes it possible for the system to display contents properly on web browsers. The answer lies on the ability to identify browser and platform information across the

7

internet. Just like other PHP procedures, the identification process takes credit from some environment variables set by PHP. Seeing these environment variables

HTTP_USER_AGENT

This environment variable is the main identifier that notes down the user's operating system and internet browser used. This variable works with another function called *getenv()*.

Getenv()

getenv() fetches the information collected by HTTP_USER_AGENT code. obtaining this information allows the system to deliver dynamic contents according to the type of browser generate. An example of the code generated for this function is:

```php
<html>
<body>
<?php
    $viewer = getenv("HTTP_USER_AGENT");
    $browser = "An unknown browser";
    if (preg_match("/MSIE/i", "$viewer"))
    {
        $browser = "Internet Explorer"
    }
    else if (preg_match("/Mozilla/i", "$viewer"))
    {
        $browser = "Mozilla";
    }
```

```
    $platform = "An unknown OS!";
    if(preg_match("/Linux/i", "$viewer"))
    {
        $platform = "Linux!";
    }
    else if (preg_match( "/Windows/i", "$viewer"))
    {
        $platform = "Windows!";
    }
    echo ("Visitor is using $browser on $platform");
?>
</body>
</html>
```

This code possesses special conditional statements like if-else statements, which you'll learn in the next chapters in this book. What this code commands is to display the detected platform and browser version according to the data gathered. This code is divided into two sets. The first parts with *if* statements identify the browser and operating system. The next parts utilize *else* statements, which means code should display the information if the condition is other than what the if statement has stated. Translating this into code, the browser part means that if the detected browser is MSIE, the code should declare that the user is using Internet Explorer for a browser. If the detected value didn't match the first if statement, it should compare the value of the next statements then declare them accordingly. The same thing happens in identifying operating system.

Finally, the *echo* part will display the declared value according to the derived data from the user support. Once it detected the browser and platform, it will display:

"Visitor is using Mozilla on Windows"

Knowing this information lets the system display images and other files properly without worrying about possible browser-level inconsistencies

Other Web Browser Functions as Supported by PHP

PHP with HTML makes it possible for you to access your web browser data and other online programs according to their build. Behind the HTML code lies the PHP functions that draw random images displayed on the web browser, html forms, browser redirection, using file download box, and a lot more.

Code Commenting

If you have tried checking out some PHP codes before online, you probably see some of them with written notes explaining what the syntax do for the project. This process is called commenting. However, codes are also made of different words, which means writing codes is not as simple as typing the words on the same platform. PHP might read the comments as part of the codes and may cause inconsistencies in the coding since the system doesn't recognize the used syntaxes.

The Impotence of Commenting

Commenting is important in creating codes. Studying PHP means you'll be dealing with codes upon beginning your studies. Even if you spend a week in mastering a code, there's a chance that you will forget what you did for that particular lesson. Use comments as way to remind you of what the code is until you can master without the need for notes.

Aside from being reminders, comments can also be used for noting down your insights in doing the project. You probably learned some insights along the way that you might want to note down immediately. Writing them on a separate note is possible, but you might want to write them right beside the code that teaches you the lesson learned along the way.

Comment Styles

Commenting will require you to use two slashes before the first word for your comment. Two slashes are indicators that the comments are not parts of the codes and won't show any error messages. Let's take the first code used in this chapter and comment on them:

```php
<?php
    $viewer = getenv("HTTP_USER_AGENT");
    // This is your comment.
?>
```

Using the slashes guarantee that your comments won't get in the way of the code's process. The aforementioned code used is called a one-line comment. You can also use multi-line comment if you have long notes to write and you want to organize them on multiple lines. Write your multi-line comment by starting with a slash then asterisk. Since you have a long comment, you need to close it by typing asterisk then slash. For example:

```php
<?php
    $viewer = getenv("HTTP_USER_AGENT");
    /* This is your multi-line comment.
```

Type several words as you want.

Enclose your comment in asterisk and a slash. */

```
?>
```

Writing multi-line comments can confuse the system, which is why it needs to be enclosed in the aforementioned character. This lets the system know that not all the lines in the comments are part of the main codes. Consider them as parentheses alerting the platform that their content is excluded from the actual code. Be careful in writing down comments because forgetting to type these characters can cause problematic codes and affect the process you're trying to build.

Coding Standard

Coding in PHP may seem like slabbing words and characters on the platform. However, PHP developers also create specific coding standards to create consistency across the groups of individuals using the coding system. Several reasons trigger the importance of following a specific coding standard:

- New programmers' tendency to change codes without following standardized coding procedures. Hence, people checking the main source code will become unmanageable.
- Code organization. Going with the standard coding makes them easier to look at.
- Organized code will also help others understand the code you created in case they will need to check them out as reference or for modification.
- You'll also find your code easier to understand and master them faster. Scanning and finding possible

mistakes also become easier by following a specific code standard.

- Maintaining a code standard also aids in developing top quality program, which developers make as their brand.

Several Points to Remember in Coding Standards

Codes created come with numerous characters, which implies that the standards will include how the characters are going to be presented on the platform, acceptable characters to use, construction and a lot more.

PHP Code Tags

Using the code *<?php* and ending it with *?>* is a must. This code is part of the PHP compliance that ensure PHP codes will be integrated and working on a wide array of operating systems and platforms. Some people use shorthand version *<? ?>*, which is unacceptable and may cause inconsistencies on some platforms. Placing this code version should be:

```
<?php
   All other codes here.
?>
```

Control Structures

Arranging control statements (*if, while, switch*, etc.) must be carefully placed or else the platform won't be able to read it. The main rule is placing a space between the opening parenthesis and the statement keyword. This differentiates control statements from functions. Curly braces must also be used even if adding them can be optional. See how this rule applies on this code:

```
if ((state1) || (state2)) {
   action1;
```

```
} elseif ((state3) && (state4)) {

  action2;

} else {

  default action;

}
```

Functions and Definitions

Functions' structures vary depending whether you're declaring a function or if you're setting up its definition. Function calls should have no space between the function keyword and the open parenthesis. They, however, parameters used inside the parenthesis must be followed by commas and have spaces. The last parameter, though, doesn't need to have comma or spaces. Just close the parameter list with closing parenthesis. For example:

```
$var = func($parameter1, $parameter2, $parameter3);
```

When it comes to declaration or definitions, functions will have a nested set of codes applying the same rules. See how a combination of a function call and definition, which uses an *if* statement, is coded in this example:

```
function func($parameter1, $parameter2 = ")

{

  if (condition) {

    statement;

  }

  return $val;

}
```

Variable Naming Rules

Variables serve as identifiers. Every variable will be declared with a specific value, which will be used later on coding. To make variables function accordingly, programmers must follow coding standards for representation.

Variable names should be in lower case letters and separated by "_" if necessary. The underline will serve as space. Using an actual space won't work because the platform doesn't support it for programming. Static variables must have "s" must be placed at the beginning of the indicator.

Global variables and constants also come with their own standards. Global constants also use "_" as separator. Constants should have "g" at the beginning of the indicator.

Indentation and Line Length

Seeing the codes will give you an idea that indentation will be used in coding. The typical indent should be four spaces. You might find using tab more convenient since it will create an indent without pressing the space bar several times. However, don't use tab because tab settings vary across operating systems. Even if your tab is set to move four spaces, it may not be the same with other users' settings. This messes up coding and won't show the same result that you had on your own system.

Code length is also important for organization purposes. A line of codes should only have around 75 to 85 characters. This makes code reading easier and more convenient to scan for possible mistakes.

Chapter 3: PHP Basics

This chapter will teach you the primary things that you need to know when starting to code PHP. It includes PHP's syntax rules, variables, constants, echo and print, operators, and superglobals.

Syntax

PHP code can be placed anywhere in an HTML document or it can be saved in a file with .php as its file extension. Just like JavaScript, you will need to enclose PHP code inside tags to separate it from HTML. The tag will tell browsers that all the lines inside it are PHP code.

PHP's opening tag is <?php and its closing tag is ?>. For example:

```
<!DOCTYPE html>
</html>
<head></head>
<body>
    <h1>Heading for the page</h2>
    <p>Some paragraph</p>
    <?php
        // Insert some PHP code in here.
    ?>
</body>
</html>
```

Echo and Print

PHP code blocks do not only return the values you requested from them, but you can also let it return HTML or text to the HTML file that invoked the PHP code blocks. To do that, you will need to use the echo or print command. Below are samples on how they can be used:

```
<?php

echo "Hello World!";

?>

<?php

print "Hello World!";

?>
```

Once the browser parses that part of the HTML, that small code will be processed on the server, and the server will send the value "Hello World" back to the client. Browsers handle echo and print values by placing them in the HTML file code. It will appear after the HTML element where the PHP code was inserted. For example:

```
<p>This is a paragraph.</p>

<?php

echo "Hello World!";

?>

<p>This is another paragraph.</p>
```

Once the browser parses those lines, this will be the result:

This is a paragraph.

Hello World!

This is another paragraph.

You can even echo HTML elements. For example:

```
<p>P1.</p>
<?php
print "<a href='http://www.google.com' >Google</a>";
?>
<p>P2.</p>
```

As you have witnessed, both echo and print have identical primary function, which is to send output to the browser. They have two differences however. Print can only handle one parameter while echo can handle multiple parameters. Another difference is that you can use print in expressions since it returns a value of 1 while you cannot use echo. Below is a demonstration of their differences:

```
<?php
echo "Hello World!", "How are you?";
?>
<?php
print "Hello World!", "How are you?";
?>
```

The echo code will be successfully sent to the client, but the print code will bring up a syntax error due to the unexpected comma (,) and the additional parameter or value after it. Though, if you want to use print with multiple parameters, you can concatenate the values of the parameters instead. String concatenation will be discussed later.

```
<?php
$x = 1 + print("test");
```

```php
echo $x;

?>

<?php

$x = 1 + echo("test");

echo $x;

?>
```

The variable $x will have a value of 2 since the expression print("test") will return a value of 1. Also, even it is used as a value in an expression, the print command will still produce an output.

On the other hand, the echo version of the code will return a syntax error due to the unexpected appearance of echo in the expression.

Many web developers use the echo and print commands to provide dynamic web content for small and simple projects. In advanced projects, using return to send an array of variables that contain HTML content and displaying them using JavaScript or any client side scripting is a much better method.

Variables

Creating a variable in JavaScript requires you to declare it and use the keyword var. In PHP, you do not need to declare to create a variable. All you need to do is assign a value in a variable for it to be created. Also, variables in PHP always starts with a dollar sign ($).

```php
<?php

$examplevariable = "Hello World!";

echo $examplevariable;
```

?>

There are rules to follow when creating a variable, which are similar to JavaScript's variable syntax.

➢ *The variable's name or identifier must start with a dollar sign ($).*

➢ *An underscore or a letter must follow it.*

➢ *Placing a number or any symbol after the dollar sign instead will return a syntax error.*

➢ *The identifier must only contain letters, numbers, or underscores.*

➢ *Identifiers are case sensitive. The variable $x is treated differently from $X.*

You can assign any type of data into a PHP variable. You can store strings, integers, floating numbers, and so on. If you have experienced coding using other programming languages, you might be thinking where you would need to declare the data type of the variable. You do not need to do that. PHP will handle that part for you. All you need to do is to assign the values in your variables.

Variable Scopes

Variables in PHP also change their scope, too, depending on the location where you created them.

Local

If you create a variable inside a function, it will be treated as a local variable. Unlike JavaScript, assigning a value to variable for the first time inside a function will not make them global due to way variables are created in PHP.

Global

If you want to create global variables, you can do it by creating a value outside your script's functions. Another method is to use the global keyword. The global keyword can let you create or access global variables inside a function. For example:

```php
<?php
function test() {
    global $x;
    $x = "Hello World!";
}
test();
echo $x;
?>
```

In the example above, the line global $x defined variable $x as a global variable. Because of that, the echo command outside the function was able to access $x without encountering an undefined variable error.

As mentioned a while ago, you can use the global keyword to access global variables inside functions. Below is an example:

```php
<?php
$x = "Hello Word!";
function test() {
    global $x;
    echo $x;
}
```

```
test();
?>
```

Just like before, the command echo will not encounter an error as long as the global keyword was used for the variable $x.

Another method you can use is to access your script's global values array, $GLOBALS. With $GLOBALS, you can create or access global values. Here is the previous example used once again, but with the $GLOBALS array used instead of the global keyword:

```
<?php
function test() {
        $GLOBALS['x'] = "Hello World!";
}
test();
echo $x;
?>
```

Take note that when using $GLOBALS, you do not need the dollar sign when creating or accessing a variable.

Static

If you are not comfortable in using global variables just to keep the values that your functions use, you can opt to convert your local variables to static. Unlike local variables, static variables are not removed from the memory once the function that houses them ends. They will stay in the memory like global variables, but they will be only accessible on the functions they reside in. For example:

```
<?php
```

```
function test() {
        static $y = 1;
        if (empty($y))
                {$y = 1;}
        echo $y . " ";
        $y += $y;
}
test();
test();
test();
test();
test();
?>
```

In the example, the variable $y's value is expected to grow double as the function is executed. With the help of static keyword, the existence and value of $y is kept in the script even if the function where it serves as a local variable was already executed.

As you can see, together with the declaration that the variable $y is static, the value of 1 was assigned to it. The assignment part in the declaration will only take effect during the first time the function was called and the static declaration was executed.

Superglobals

PHP has predefined global variables. They contain values that are commonly accessed, define, and manipulated in everyday server side data execution. Instead of manually capturing those values, PHP has placed them into its predefined superglobals to make the life of PHP programmers easier.

- ➤ *$GLOBALS*
- ➤ *$_SERVER*
- ➤ *$_REQUEST*
- ➤ *$_POST*
- ➤ *$_GET*
- ➤ *$_FILES*
- ➤ *$_ENV*
- ➤ *$_COOKIE*
- ➤ *$_SESSION*

Superglobals have CORE USES IN PHP SCRIPTING. YOU WILL BE MOSTLY USING ONLY FIVE OF THESE SUPERGLOBALS IN YOUR EARLY DAYS IN CODING PHP. THEY ARE: $GLOBALS, $_SERVER, $_REQUEST, $_POST, AND $_GET.

Constants

Constants are data storage containers just like variables, but they have global scope and can be assigned a value once. Also, the method of creating a constant is much different than creating a variable. When creating constants, you will need to use the define() construct. For example:

```php
<?php
define(this_is_a_constant, "the value", false);
?>
```

The define() construct has three parameters: define(name of constant, value of the constant, is case sensitive?). A valid constant name must start with a letter or an underscore – you do not need to place a dollar sign ($) before it. Aside from that, all other naming rules of variables apply to constants.

The third parameter requires a Boolean value. If the third parameter was given a true argument, constants can be accessed regardless of their case or capitalization. If set to false, its case will be strict. By default, it will be set to false.

Operators

By time, you must be already familiar with operators, so this book will only refresh you about them. Fortunately, the usage of operators in JavaScript and PHP is almost similar.

- ➢ *Arithmetic: +, -, *, /, %, and **.*

- ➢ *Assignment: =, +=, -=, *=, /=, and %=.*

- ➢ *Comparison: ==, ===, !=, <>, !==, >, <, >=, and <=.*

- ➢ *Increment and Decrement: ++x, x++, --x, and x--.*

- ➢ *Logical: and, or, xor, &&, ||, and !.*

- ➢ *String: . and .=.*

- ➢ *Array: +, ==, ===, !=, <>, and !==.*

Chapter 4: Flow Control

Flow control is needed when advancing or creating complex projects with any programming language. With them, you can control the blocks of statements that will be executed in your script or program. Most of the syntax and rules in the flow control constructs in PHP are almost similar to JavaScript, so you will not have a hard time learning to use them in your scripts.

Functions

Along the way, you will need to create functions for some of the frequently repeated procedures in your script. Creating functions in PHP is similar to JavaScript. The difference is that function names in PHP are not case sensitive. For example:

```php
<?php

function test($parameter = "no argument input") {

    print $parameter;

}

TEST("Success!");

tEsT();

?>
```

In JavaScript, calling a function using its name in different casing will cause an error. With PHP, you will encounter no problems or errors as long as the spelling of the name is correct.

Also, did you notice the variable assignment on the sample function's parameter? The value assigned to the parameter's purpose is to provide a default value to it when the function was called without any arguments being passed for the parameter.

In the example, the second invocation of the function test did not provide any arguments for the function to assign to the $parameter. Because of that, the value 'no argument input' was assigned to $parameter instead.

In JavaScript, providing a default value for a parameter without any value can be tricky and long depending on the number of parameters that will require default arguments or parameter values.

Of course, just like JavaScript, PHP functions also return values with the use of the return keyword.

If, Else, and Elseif Statements

PHP has the same if construct syntax as JavaScript. To create an if block, start by typing the if keyword, and then follow it with an expression to be evaluated inside parentheses. After that, place the statements for your if block inside curly braces. Below is an example:

```php
<?php
$color1 = "blue";
if ($color1 == "blue") {
    echo "The color is blue! Yay!";
}
?>
```

If you want your if statement to do something else if the condition returns a false, you can use else.

```php
<?php
$color1 = "blue";
```

```php
if ($color1 == "blue") {
    echo "The color is blue! Yay!";
}
else {
    echo "The color is not blue, you liar!";
}
?>
```

In case you want to check for more conditions in your else statements, you can use elseif instead nesting an if statement inside else. For example:

```php
<?php
$color1 = "blue";
if ($color1 == "blue") {
    echo "The color is blue! Yay!";
}
else {
    if ($color == "green") {
        echo "Hmm. I like green, too. Yay!";
    }
    else {
        echo "The color is not blue, you liar!";
    }
}
?>
```

Is the same as:

```php
<?php
$color1 = "blue";
if ($color1 == "blue") {
    echo "The color is blue! Yay!";
}
elseif ($color == "green" {
    echo "Hmm. I like green, too. Yay!";}
else {
    echo "The color is not blue, you liar!";
}
?>
```

Using elseif is less messy and is easier to read.

Switch Statement

However, if you are going to check for multiple conditions for one expression or variable and place a lot of statements per condition satisfied, it is better to use switch than if statements. For example, the previous if statement is the same as:

```php
<?php
$color1 = "blue";
switch ($color1) {
    case "blue":
        echo "The color is blue! Yay!";
        break;
```

```
    case "green":
        echo "Hmm. I like green, too. Yay!";
        break;
    case default:
        echo "The color is not blue, you liar!";
}
?>
```

The keyword switch starts the switch statement. Besides it is the value or expression that you will test. It must be enclosed in parentheses.

Every case keyword entry must be accompanied with the value that you want to compare against the expression being tested. Each case statement can be translated as if <expression 1> is equal to <expression 2>, and then perform the statements below.

The break keyword is used to signal the script that the case block is over and the any following statements after it should not be done.

On the other hand, the default case will be executed when no case statements were satisfied by the expression being tested.

While Statement

"While" statement is regarded as the simplest form of loop. A typical while statement structure includes expression and statement and constructed as:

while *(expression)*

   statement

Expression will undergo evaluation once played. If evaluation showed that the statement is "true", it's paired *statement* will be executed. *Expression* will then undergo reevaluation. Reevaluation with "true" results will once again execute the *statement*, which will continue to form a loop of flow as long as *expression* presents "true" all the time on evaluation. The loop stops or exits once evaluation results showed as "false". A simple example is this code:

```
$total = o

$a = 2;

while ($a <= 20) {

  $total += $a;

}
```

In this code, the statement will add numbers from 2 to 20 to the original number declared by $total, which is o. This loop will continue until the expression becomes false.

Coding loops using while statement lets coders explore their options when it comes to how they want the loop to run. Options include using break or coding a *do/while* loop.

Placing a break in a code instructs the loop to exit prematurely or won't complete the loop as indicated in the code. For example:

```
$total = o

$a = 2;

while ($a <= 20) {

  $total += $a;

if ($a == 10)
```

```
    break;

    $total += $a;

    $a++
}
```

In this expression, $a won't arrive at value 11 since the break code stops the loop once it reaches 10.

On the other hand, PHP lets users place a *do/while* loop that ensures the code will execute the loop at least once. This loop's structure is:

do

   statement

while (*expression*)

Applying this statement to the code above:

$total = 0

$a = 2;

do {

   $total += $a++

} while ($a <= 20);

For statements

The *for* statement is comparable to the *while* statement, but made shorter and with expressed counter elements. Its shorter coding gives way to the code being easier to read than while statements.

Structurally, a *for* statement looks like this:

for (start; condition; increment)

 statement

Code evaluation begins at the syntax start although its evaluation occurs once. Condition will be tested all the time within the loop. A true result will execute the body loop. Loop ends if the result becomes false. Increment is tested after the command loop executed.

Applying this statement in a code:

```
$total = 0
for ($a = 2; $a <= 20; $a++) {
  $total += $a;
}
```

This code follows the same process of adding numbers from 2 to 20 in while statement, but represented in for statement. Notice how the code shifted in terms of placement in the loop body because of the new labels each element obtained. Just like in while statement, break and continue syntaxes can be placed to exit a loop earlier or continue it after placing the continue code.

Foreach Statement

Foreach statement works in iterating arrays and objects. Using this statement to other variables will show errors.

Foreach statement can be represented by two syntaxes:

foreach (array_expression as $value)

    statement code to be executed

foreach (array expression as $key => $value)

    statement code to be executed

In the first code, the element's value will be attributed or assigned to the syntax $value. The internal pointer in the array will move by one, which will result to the next element's value on the next evaluation.

In the second code, the element's key will be assigned to the $key variable for every evaluation.

Customized object iteration is also possible with this statement. On the other hand, *foreach statement* automatically resets the initial or first array element, which means calling or coding *reset()* is unnecessary before setting *foreach* loop.

Take note of this array of odd number when this code is applied:

$arr = array (1, 3, 5);

foreach ($arr as &$value) {

    $value = $value * 2;

}

Array iteration in this set changes the array into (2, 5, 10) because of the set value multiplied by 2.

Chapter 5: Data Types – Part 1

PHP also has the same data types that you can create and use in other programming languages. Some of the data types in PHP have different ways of being created and assigned from the data types in JavaScript.

Strings

Any character or combination of characters placed in double or single quotes are considered strings in PHP. In PHP, you will deal with text a lot more often than other programming languages. PHP is used typically to handle data going from the client to the server and vice versa.   Due to that, you must familiarize yourself with a few of the most common used string operators and methods.

Numbers

Integer

Integers are whole numbers without fractional components or values after the decimal value. When assigning or using integers in PHP, it is important that you do not place blanks and commas between them to denote or separate place values.

An integer value can be positive, negative or zero. In PHP, you can display integers in three forms: decimal (base 10), octal (base 8), or hexadecimal (base 16). To denote that a value is in hexadecimal form, always put the prefix 0x (zero-x) with the value (e.g., 0x1F, 0x4E244D, 0xFF11AA). On the other hand, to denote that a value is in octal form, put the prefix 0 (zero) with the value (e.g., 045, 065, and 0254).

If you echo or print an integer variable, its value will be automatically presented in its decimal form. In case that you want to show it in hexadecimal or octal you can use dechex() or decoct() respectively. For example:

```php
<?php
echo dechex(255);
echo decoct(9);
?>
```

The first echo will return FF, which is 255 in decimal. The second echo will return 11, which is 9 in octal. As you might have noticed, the prefix 0x and 0 were not present in the result. The prefixes only apply when you write those two presentations of integers in your script.

On the other hand, you can use hexdec() to reformat a hexadecimal value to decimal and use octdec() to reformat an octal value to decimal.

You might think of converting hex to oct or vice versa. Unfortunately, PHP does not have constructs like hexoct() or octhex(). To perform that kind of operation, you will need to manually convert the integer to decimal first then convert it to hex or oct.

Float or Double

Floating numbers are real numbers (or approximations of real numbers). In other words, it can contain fractional decimal values.

Since integers are a subset of real numbers, integers are floating numbers. Just adding a decimal point and a zero to an integer in PHP will make PHP consider that the type of the variable that will store that value is float instead of integer.

Boolean

Boolean is composed of two values: True and False. In PHP, true and false are not case sensitive. Both values are used primarily in conditional statements, just like in JavaScript.

Also, false is equivalent to null, a blank string, and 0 while true is equivalent to any number except 0 or any string that contains at least one character.

NULL

This is a special value type. In case that a variable does not contain a value from any other data types, it will have a NULL value instead. For example, if you try to access a property from an object that has not been assigned a value yet, it will have a NULL value. By the way, you can assign NULL to variables, too.

Resource

Resources is a special variable type. They only serve as a reference to external resource and are only created by special functions. An example of a resource is a database link.

Chapter 6: Data Types – Part 2

The data types explained in this chapter are essential to your PHP programming life. In other programming languages, you can live without this data types. However, in PHP, you will encounter them most of the time, especially if you will start to learn and use databases on your scripts.

ARRAYS

Arrays are data containers for multiple values. You can store numbers, strings, and even arrays in an array. Array in PHP is a tad different in JavaScript, so it will be discussed in detail in this book.

There are three types of array in PHP: indexed, associative, and multidimensional.

Indexed Arrays

Indexed array is the simplest form of arrays in PHP. For those people who are having a hard time understanding arrays, think of an array as a numbered list that starts with zero. To create or assign values to an array, you must use the construct array(). For example:

```php
<?php

$examplearray = array(1, 2, "three");

?>
```

To call values inside an array, you must call them using their respective indices. For example:

```php
<?php

$examplearray = array(1, 2, "three");

echo $examplearray[0];
```

```
echo $examplearray['2'];
?>
```

The first echo will reply with 1 and the second echo will reply three. As you can see, in indexed arrays, you can call values with just a number or a number inside quotes. When dealing with indexed arrays, it is best that you use the first method.

Since the number 1 was the first value to be assigned to the array, index 0 was assigned to it. The index number of the values in an array increment by 1. So, the index numbers of the values 2 and three are 1 and 2 respectively.

Associative Arrays

The biggest difference between associative arrays and indexed arrays is that you can define the index keys of the values in associative arrays. The variable $GLOBALS is one of the best example of associative arrays in PHP. To create an associative array, follow the example:

```
<?php
$examplearray = array("index0" => "John", 2 => "Marci");
echo $examplearray["index0"];
echo $examplearray[2];
?>
```

The first echo will return John and the second echo will return Marci. Take note that if you use associative array, the values will not have indexed numbers.

Multidimensional Arrays

Multidimensional arrays can store values, indexed arrays, and associative arrays. If you create an array in your script, the $GLOBALS variable will become a multidimensional array. You can insert indexed or associative arrays in multidimensional arrays. However, take note that the same rules apply to their index keys. To create one, follow the example below:

```php
<?php
$examplearray = array(array("test1", 1, 2), array("test2" =>
3, "test3" => 4), array("test4", 5, 6));
echo $examplearray[1]["test2"];
echo $examplearray[1][1];
echo $examplearray[2][0];
?>
```

As you can see, creating multidimensional arrays is just like nesting arrays on its value. Calling values from multidimensional is simple.

If a value was assigned, it can be called like a regular array value using its index key. If a value was paired with a named key, it can be called by its name. If an array was assigned, you can call the value inside it by calling the index key of the array first, and then the index key of the value inside it.

In the example, the third echo called the array in index 2 and accessed the value located on its 0 index. Hence, it returned test4.

Objects

Objects are like small programs inside your script. You can assign variables within them called properties. You can also assign functions within them called methods.

Creating and using objects can make you save hundreds of lines of code, especially if you have some bundle of codes that you need to use repeatedly on your scripts. To be on the safe side, the advantages of using objects depend on the situation and your preferences.

Debates about using objects in their scripts (object oriented programming) or using functions (procedural programming) instead have been going on forever. It is up to you if you will revolve your programs around objects or not.

Nevertheless, to create objects, you must create a class for them first. Below is an example on how to create a class in PHP.

```php
<?php
class Posts {
    function getPost() {
        $this->post1 = "Post Number 1.";
    }
    var $post2 = "Post Number 2.";
}


$test = new Posts();
echo $test->post2;
$test->getPost();
echo $test->post1;
?>
```

In this example, a new class was created using the class keyword. The name of the class being created is Posts. In class declarations, you can create functions that will be methods for the objects under the class. And you can create variables that will be properties for the subjects under the class.

First, a function was declared. If the function was called, it will create a property for an object under the Posts class called post1. Also, a value was assigned to it. You might have noticed the $this part in the declaration inside the function. The $this variable represents the object that owns the function being declared.

Besides it is a dash and a chevron (->). Some programmers informally call it as the instance operator. This operator allows access to the instances (methods and properties) of an object. In the statement, the script is accessing the post1 property inside the $this object, which is the object that owns the function. After accessing the property, the statement assigned a value to it.

Aside from the function or method declaration, the script created a property called post2, which is a variable owned by the Posts class. To declare one, you need to use the keyword var (much like in JavaScript). After this statement, the class declaration ends.

The next statement contains the variable assignment, $test = new Posts(). Technically, that means that the variable $test will become a new object under the Posts class. All the methods and properties that was declared inside the Posts() class declaration will be given to it.

To test if the $test class became a container for a Posts object, the script accessed the property post2 from $test and then echoed it to produce an output. The echo will return , 'Post number 2.'. Indeed, the $test variable is already an object under the Posts class.

What if you call and print the property post1 from the variable $test? It will not return anything since it has not been created or initialized yet. To make it available, you need to invoke the getPost() method of $test. Once you do, you will be able to access the property post1.

And that is just the tip of the iceberg. You will be working more on objects on advanced PHP projects.

Chapter 7: File Manipulation and Operations

PHP programming today can work on database for storing data within the server or web host. However, some web hosts doesn't allow clients to store database, which makes file manipulation knowledge via PHP handy for programmers.

Through this section, you'll discover how to open, create and edit files via PHP programming.

Before getting into the technical aspect, you must understand first the concept of file manipulation in PHP. The concept is the same as accessing data in your computer. Load or open the file first and decide whether you just want to read the contents, write additional information, or edit the current contents in a file. Once done, close the file and continue with the rest of the procedure needed for programming. Just the same, every file operation command has its own mode that can be useful for users.

Opening a File

The *fopen()* function opens a file, a link or URL. This process works with the designated file then brings it into a stream and load. Coding this command includes the following syntaxes:

```
<?php

$handle = fopen(filename.ext)

?>
```

In this code, the filename refers to the file's saved name while ext. is the extension name. Common practices include manipulating text (.txt) files, but you'll also learn how to manipulate comma-separated values (.csv) files, which can be imported as spreadsheet or database files.

Type the code as is in opening files within the same directory. In opening files in a different folder or drive, type the destination site to open.

```php
<?php

$handle = fopen("c:\\folder name\\filename.ext);

fclose($handle);

?>
```

If you are familiar with command prompt, you've probably tried accessing some files and folders through this syntax. Double forward slashes indicate the path. They serve as separators to indicate whether the file is within the folder or if it's the file itself. in this code, the file filename.ext is inside the folder name, which is one of the folders in C drive.

You can also type extra letters to manipulate the file. Integrating these new processes mean the platform should open the file and follow it with the next procedure like read or write.

Most people would think that opening is equivalent to reading, just like in opening files on OS-based platforms. However, the process of opening file is limited to setting a pointer to the file you wish to access. It will then return a file handle, which is important for PHP to remember the file's location.

Reading a File

Reading files can be done in several commands. This makes the file available for reading only, which means no edits or writing can be done on the file when opened. One of the codes to use in reading a file is this code:

```php
<?PHP
    $file_contents = readfile("filename.ext");
    print $file_contents;
?>
```

Using this code will launch the file into web page with texts without commas separating the contents. This code can also be minimized into one line if preferred:

```php
print readfile("filename.ext");
```

But looking closely at the command, the syntax *$file_content = readfile("filename.ext");* is the code that actually reads the contents. Codes used for this operation will also work using a variable if you want to train your coding procedures. Be sure to declare the variable's value properly for the platform to read it accordingly.

```php
$file_to_read = "filename.ext";
```

```php
print readfile(filename.ext)
```

Utilizing *fopen()* function to read a file requires appending "*r*" or "*r+*". "*r*" is appended to the command to read only the file and place the pointer right at the beginning of the data. Using "*r+*" means the file will be opened for reading and writing with the pointer placed at the beginning of the file. Code it this way.

```php
<?php
$handle = fopen("filename.ext", "r")
?>
```

```php
<?php
$handle = fopen("filename.ext", "r+")
```

?>

Writing on a File

Writing on a file requires you to know your main goal in accessing the file. Goals include writing on a file by appending additional information or clearing the entire file out. This will keep you from overwriting file contents and possible inconsistencies in the platform.

Writing files for PHP can vary depending on the type of PHP version used. PHP versions lower than PHP 5 can use the *fwrite()* as the main function joined together with *fopen()*.

As mentioned earlier, you must know whether you want to append contents or overwrite the current contents of the file. Your writing to file goal affects the types of syntax to use.

Writing on file will use the letters "*w*" or "*w+*". "*w*" will only write contents into a file. It will remove all the current contents and replace them with the new contents indicated. "w+" allows users to write on the file and read the file as well. Coding them to write to file includes these syntaxes:

```php
<?PHP
    $file_handle = fopen("filename.ext". "w");
    $file_contents = "Example texts";


    fwrite($file_handle, $file_contents);
    fclose($file_handle);
    print "file generated and noted to";
?>
```

The first line requires PHP to load the file. In case the file name entered doesn't exist in the folder or drive, PHP will create it for you as a new file. Notice that there's the "w" syntax on the command, which can be "w+" if you prefer PHP to read it as well. Creating a file handle means creating a pointer to the file, which is filename.ext, in this case.

The third line is where the writing process occurs. The first entry is the file that you want to tweak or to write on to, and the second one is the content that you want to enter. Try coding this command and the file with your chosen filename will be created.

Pairing up with the "w" modes are the "a" modes. PHP programming doesn't really indicate what the letter means, but it is probably obtained from its function--appending contents into an existing file. If you write "a" instead of "w" on the command, the code won't delete the contents. Rather, it will place the file pointer at the last end of contents or file. Using this command merely adds contents without doing anything on the pre-existing content placed earlier. This goes the same for "*a+*" mode. It lets you append content while reading the contents in the code.

Regardless of the difference, using "*a*" modes has a similarity with "*w*" mode in terms of file creation. Both will let you create a file in case the filename requested is non-existent in the folder.

Try playing around with the code above by interchanging "*w*" and "*a*" modes. You'll notice their effects on existing codes and will help you enhance the content according to your preference.

Other important modes are "*x*" and "*c*" modes. "*x*" modes are used for creating a new file. Sometimes, programmers forget that they already have the file created earlier. This is comparative to the OS-based feature where the document processing software will notify you that a file of the same name is already existent. In PHP, the "*x*" mode will give a false result and warning. In case the file is non-existent, it will create the file and continue with the writing process.

"*c*" modes, on the other hand, don't function the same as the "*w*" and "*x*" in terms of truncating files or sending warning messages. However, these modes are ideal for those wishing to get *flock()* function prior to file modification. *flock()* is also known as advisory lock that creates a simple RW model that can be accessed or used on almost every platform. Just the same, adding plus signs to these functions will make them read or write the file.

As mentioned earlier, the first code is used for below PHP 5 versions. Writing on PHP 5 requires users to use *file_put_contents()* instead of *fwrite()*. The only similarity is they will be placed on the same third line as *fwrite()*. Changing the texts will then make it into *file_put_contents($file_handle, $file_contents, context)*. Using this function will change the type of codes used for the version available. Options include:

file_use_include_path

file_append

lock_ex.

CSV File and Manipulation in PHP

A CSV file is often used in many online database and can be exported to spreadsheet file. However, viewing this file on a text editor will show a series of item separated by commas. Separating information with a comma means it will be placed on the first row, the second data is placed on the second row, and so on. To give you an example, here's how it look like on text and once exported into spreadsheet. Below is a product list with quantity number and total prices saved as .csv file and viewed in text and spreadsheet file.

- card, 1, $1
- pencil, 2, $3
- eraser, 4, $2

When viewed in a spreadsheet document, it looks like this:

	A	B	C
1	card	1	$1
2	pencil	2	$3
3	eraser	4	$2

In PHP, you will not work on .csv file as seen on spreadsheet, but as text file. You will work with commas in designating values to each spreadsheet and cells by using the function *fgetcsv()*. Using this function lets you gather data and arrange them into an array. The code to use includes the following:

```
<?PHP

    $file_handle = fopen("filename.ext", "r");

    while (!feof($file_handle)) {

        $line_of_data                    =
fgetcsv($file_handle,size_of_line);

        print
$line_of_data[0].$line_of_data[1].$line_of_data[2].
"<BR>";

    }
```

fclose($file_handle);

?>

Just like in other codes, several processes occurred in typing this .csv code. The first two line, which are also used in other codes, is setting handle for the file. The *while statement* will create a loop for both data and code.

On the third line is the *fgetcsv()* function that will be used in gathering data and setting them into an array. notice that the parenthesis after fgetcsv has two value: the file handle and the size of line. the size of the line is self-explanatory. this value may vary depending on the size of data to read. there's no actual value placed becuase it will depend on your data and editable.

The next set of code is the *$line_of_data* code. This is the variable used to represent the line of text within the .csv data that you're planning to launch on your webpage. *$line_of_data* can be changed depending on how you want it to be represented on the code. In previous example, *$line_of_data* is the value separated by comma as shown above. What makes this function intelligent is it will split the line upon seeing the comma separator. It will generate the data and arrange them into the array. Hence, displaying the numbers with brackets. The function arranges the data as:

$line_of_data[0]

$line_of_data[1]

$line_of_data[2]

Again, the number of data to be arranged on an array is not limited to three. It can be extended depending on the size of line that you want to be printed. Using the print function will display the value on their respective array and will be displayed on the webpage as a .csv file. Since the appearance of this data listing can be quite confusing, programmers often use HTML line break to make it easier to read once published online.

Setting Data in an Array

CSV manipulation is already a helpful procedure for programmers in setting up data in arrays. Nevertheless, there are still other ways on how to set it up through other functions like *explode()*. This creates an array according to each text line indicated in the data. Codes for this process are:

```
<?PHP
    $fine_handle = fopen("filename.ext", "rb");
    while (!feof($file_handle)) {
        $line_of_data = fgets($file_handle);
        $parts = explode('=', $line_of_data);
        print $parts[0] . $parts[1]. "<BR>";
    }
    fclose($file_handle);
?>
```

Examine this code. Instead of using *fgetcsv()*, the code utilizes *fgets()*, the function used for fetching line from a file pointer. The process still follows except for some noticeable changes in the syntax. It will also get the file hander and use while loop. One of the difference is the use of "*rb*", where in r makes it reading possible. "*b*" is the mode that forces a file to open in binary mode. Binary mode, a common term in programming and computing, means a unit will only have two possible states, represented by 1 and 0. Several platforms recognize both binary modes and others, which highlights the significance of using "b" and force to open the file in binary mode. In this case, the file is going to be read into binary mode.

The *explode()* function after *fgets()* lets you separate a line of data according to your used separator. As you can see, separators used for data in PHP don't have to be commas all the time. It also depends on how data should be presented according to preference. In this case, "=" is used as the separator of the data. For example, your file may have this kind of data:

AR = Arkansas

CA = California

NY = New York

In this data, equal sign separates state abbreviations from the actual state names. Using *explode()* function will separate the data into parts, represented by the code *$part*. This data, discarding the separator, has two rows of data that will be arranged in the array. The abbreviation part is assigned as *$parts[0]* and the *$part[1]* for the actual state names. The print function will print the data as indicated in the array. Through the coded *while* loop statement, the PHP will read the next text line and do the same process of arranging them in an array the printing.

Understanding the process of manipulating data and files with PHP is rewarding for every novice programmer. Practice these procedures for yourself and see how they work for you as a programmer.

Chapter 8: Additional Codes and Functions that will be Useful in the Long Run

PHP coding includes a lot of codes and knowing some of them can be additional skills to learn. They may not sound something that a beginner should dabble with initially. Nonetheless, they are considered as investment in the PHP learning process. You may also notice some HTML code that comes with the PHP codes, but those won't be discussed in detail on this lesson.

Date-related Functions

Programmers use two date-related functions obtain date and time values.

Date()

In the *date()*, you will generate the date for a specific time using various characters inside the parenthesis. For example:

```php
<?php
$today = date('d-m-y')
print $today
?>
```

In this syntax, the code will print the date according to the set "d-m-y" pattern. D, m, and y stand for date, month and year, respectively. However, derived value is going to be presented in numerical format. So, if the date will be displayed as 02-01-2014. Generating this information is easy, but confusing due to the differences in date format known worldwide. Looking at the data, people will think of it as either month or day first like in the case of British users where the date format starts with day while other countries use months first. Coding strategies will make the derived data more understandable for specific group of people using the function.

Utilizing the function requires a separator for displaying the derived data. This code's advantage is programmers can use different separators according to their preference. Take note of the separators used in the following codes:

$today = date('d~m~y')

$today = date('d m y')

$today = date('d:m:y')

Using this function is more about knowing the fundamentals and play around with various combination for consistency and ease of coding. The only crucial point to remember is using single quotation marks for the date format parameter. Forgetting to place these quotes will display errors.

Manipulating date function requires knowing several characters that help in displaying date values. Programmers can memorize these characters or not, but it will be handy to have a list of the code. Characters are divided into four types: the year characters, day of the week characters, time characters and other characters. See the table of the characters used in each type:

Types	Characters	Meaning	Example
Year Characters	y	Double-digit year value	01, 02, 03
	Y	Four-digit year value	2011, 2012, 2013
	L	Leap year?	1 if the answer is

			yes; 0 if no
Day of the Week Characters	w	Day of week, numeric form	0 is Sunday; 1 is Monday; 2 is Tuesday; and so on
	W	Week number	25th day of the year
	S	Ordinal ending for a month's day	3rd, 4th, 31st
	z	Numeric day of the year	0 to 365
	d	Day of the month, with zeroes	06, 07, 08
	j	Day, without zeroes	6, 7, 8
	D	Day, shortened text format	Mon, Tue, Wed
	l	Day, complete word	Monday, Tuesday, Wednesday
Time Characters	s	Seconds	00 to 59
	i	Minutes	Same as above
	a	Morning/Afternoon	am or pm
	A	Same with "a", uppercase	AM or PM
	H	24-hour format	00 to 23

	G	24-hour format, without zeroes at the beginning	0, 1, 2
	h	12-hour format	01 to 12
	g	12-hour format, without zeroes at the beginning	1, 2, 3
Other Time Characters	T	Time zone of computer	EST, PST, GMT
	O	Greenwich Meantime offset	+0300
	r	Full formatted time and date	Mon, 10 Feb 2011 16:26:44 +0300

Have this table handy and practice them in coming up with your date function scripts. Using specific characters with the function affect the printing process for displayed. Take note of the following examples:

Derive the date value using the following characters in the function:

```php
<?php

    $today = date('D F d Y');

    print $today;

    /*Date is printed with the name of day in shortened
form,
```

month in complete word, day in numeric form with zero,

*and complete year. For example, Mon January 01 2014 */*

?>

See how the date was printed in the comment. Using another character and combination may display Monday January 1 2014 or Monday 1st January 2014, etc.Iit's all about how you combine the characters.

Notice that the separator used for this set are spaces and it's not an issue with this function. You will also use the same function with time value characters in printing time values. See this code:

```php
<?php
    $time = date('h:i:s a');

    print $time;

    // Time displayed is going to be in hh:mm:ss am/pm form. For example, 10:05:35 am.

?>
```

Read the comment and see how the time value is presented. Just like in date, you can manipulate the characters to display the time together with their time zones.

Using the *date()* function depends on character usage. Nevertheless, remember that some of the characters may only be available in specific PHP versions. For instance, the character "W" is only available in version 4.1.0 and later.

Understanding the concept of date function is essential because of its role in using another date function, *getdate()*.

Getdate() Function

The *getdate()* function is also an essential date and time function to use in PHP. Unlike the regular date function, *getdate()* helps in generating an array complete with time and date values, which are often used for date comparison. A good example is comparing the number of days have passed after a given date. The code to use is:

getdate(time_stamp);

The parameter "timestamp" inside the parenthesis can be blank if preferred, but it will display the current date and time's values. The array of information includes the following presented in their numeric forms:

- yday - year day
- mday - day of the month
- mon - month
- wday - day of the week
- hours
- minutes
- seconds

On the other hand, some syntaxes will display date in text form like the following:

- year
- month - month in text form
- weekday - day in text form

The derived result from using this code is in associative array. Users can code the keys by placing them inside square brackets then print the values. Examples of these syntaxes are:

$today = getdate();

print $today['yday'];

print $today['mday'];

Just like in the *date()* function, programmers must not forget using single quotation marks to generate results.

Applying the concept of *getdate()* is beneficial for a lot of procedures that require knowing date records or time duration. Take the scenario of database access for example. You want to derive the number of days since an individual accessed the database. The heart of coding in this scenario is the syntax:

$access_date = date('z').

The table above states the 'z' character refers to the year day represented by number. Getting a value of 30 indicates the 30th day of the year. If your goal is comparing the last access date with the current date, use the following code:

```php
<?php
$access_date = 30;
$today = getdate();


$day_difference = $today['yday'] - $access_date;
print "Days since last access = .$day_difference";
?>
```

The *getdate* function is used to set up the data array. The *$day_difference* codeis used to compute for the number of days since the last access on the database.

Utilizing date-related functions is indeed helpful, but programmers should have good PHP reference sites to set up in the code properly and displayed according to preference.

File Inclusion

Programmers often type their codes from scratch. However, there are instances when they can add a PHP file's content before execution. Two functions let programmer do this procedure: the *require()* and the *include()* functions. File inclusion's advantage is it aids PHP in setting functions, footers, and other page elements that are cloned to other pages. Cloning website elements let web designers efficiently create new pages at a faster rate.

Include() Function

As the name implies, the function lets users include all the contents to the current file by copying them from the linked file. There's a chance of possible inconsistencies due to the copied contents. Programmers don't have to worry because the platform will show a warning, but the code will still execute.

Create a .php file first if you still don't have one saved in your server. For example, file header.php contains HTML codes that link URLs to their respective anchor texts. Contents are:

```
<a href="http://www.domain.com/index.htm">Homepage</a>
```

```
<a href="http://www.domain.com/about">About Us</a>
```

```
<a href="http://www.domain.com/contact">Contact Us</a>
```

Include the content to a new file through this code:

```
<html>
```

```
<body>

<?php include("header.php"); ?>

<p>You have included a PHP file!</p>

</body>

</html>
```

The output is having a line of linked anchor texts printed on top of the "You have included a PHP file!" text.

Require() Function

This function also does the same as *include()* function in terms of copying the file content into the php file that has the function. The difference lies in script problem handling brought by file inclusion. Instead of continuing with the execution, the function will prompt a fatal error warning that keeps the script from executing. Due to its nature, experts recommend using *require()* instead of *include()* since the script is prevented from loading. Forcing the function to load despite errors may affect the entire code.

The function will display error messages if the file attributed to the function is missing or misnamed. The error messages may be displayed in plain text or other types. Some programmers may not get any error at all. These differences are due to varying PHP server configuration. Users will know that there are problems because nothing will be printed on PHP. They can recheck the file and see if they typed a wrong file name.

Sending Emails

PHP also plays a vital role in sending email with its *mail()* function. But even before trying to send an email, check whether the feature is configured appropriately in the server. Look for the *php.ini* file inside the */etc/* folder within the server. A .ini file can be opened using a text file application like a notepad. Use the *Find* dialog box, launched by pressing "Ctrl+F", and look for [mail function] header on the .ini file.

Windows and Linux users must know the difference between the php.ini file saved in their servers. Both platforms have *SMTP* and *sendmail_from* fields. *SMTP* refers to the email server address. *sendmail_from* refers to the user's email address, which will appear as sender on emails. The differences between platform is the *sendmail_from* entry is blank for Linux and an additional directive or field is include. Unix has the *sendmail_path* field, which is not present in Windows. This part will have the sendmail application path together with switches utilized in sending emails.

Sending Plain Text Email

The simplest way of sending email is having a plain text mail utilizing the *mail()* function in PHP. It works like any other function that requires parameters. The code used for dispatching email is:

mail(to, subject, message, header, parameter);

The first three parameters are mandatory since they contain the vital information like recipient, the subject and the actual message. *Header* and *parameter* are optional. *Header* refers to sending options like CC and BCC, represented by \r\n code. *Parameter* refers to other additional parameter indicated on the send mail program.

Once the function is applied, PHP will try to dispatch an email and indicate whether the email was sent or not through Boolean terms, true and false.

The process of sending an email as a plain text is the same in declaring variables then compiling them as parameters in the mail() function. Take this code as an example:

```
<html>
<head>
<title>Sending Plain Email Text Form via PHP</title>
</head>
<body>
<?php>
     $to = "user@domain.com";
     $subject = "Your subject";
     $message= "Type any message that you want.";
     $header = "user2@domain.com. \r\n";
     $retval = mail($to, $subject, $message, $header);
     if( $retval == true );
     {
          echo "Message sent!";
     }
     else
     {
          echo "Message not sent. Try again.";
?>
</body>
</html>
```

In this case, the code will send an email to sender "user@domain.com". The subject is typed in as well as the main email body. The header states a copy of the email will be sent to an extra recipient, "user2@domain.com". At the end of the code, it utilizes *if statement* discussed in the earlier chapter. This code will send a command based on the conditional statement. If the email was sent, a specific text as confirmation should be displayed. If not, then notification that the message failed to send will display instead.

These are only a few of the many slightly complicated codes you'll learn in PHP. They take practice, but exposure to these additional codes early on is an advantage for you.

Conclusion

Thank you again for purchasing this book!

I hope this book was able to help you to learn PHP fast.

The next step is to:

Learn the other superglobals

Learn from handling in HTML, JavaScript, and PHP

Learn using MySQL

Finally, if you enjoyed this book, please take the time to share your thoughts and post a review on Amazon. We do our best to reach out to readers and provide the best value we can. Your positive review will help us achieve that. It'd be greatly appreciated!

Thank you and good luck!

Check Out My Other Books

Below you'll find some of my other popular books that are popular on Amazon and Kindle as well. Simply click on the links below to check them out. Alternatively, you can visit my author page on Amazon to see other work done by me.

Android Programming in a Day

Python Programming in a Day

C Programming Success in a Day

If the links do not work, for whatever reason, you can simply search for these titles on the Amazon website to find them.

www.ingramcontent.com/pod-product-compliance
Lightning Source LLC
Chambersburg PA
CBHW070940180526
45168CB00003B/1114